IMAGES
of America

ROUTE 66 IN
ARIZONA

On March 27, 1928, the runners in the Bunion Derby transcontinental footrace passed the general store at Flagstaff. Eventual winner Andy Payne is shown here. That day, Payne lagged 30 minutes behind leader Nestor Erickson. The runners struggled up 49 Hill, the highest altitude on the route at 7,410 feet. They had run 500 grueling miles in two weeks. (Cline Library.)

ON THE COVER: The 1972 Eagles hit "Take it Easy" put Winslow on the map. Jackson Browne and Glenn Frey wrote the song with the line, "Standin' on a corner in Winslow, Arizona." Decades before the song, this man was standing on the corner at Second Street and Kinsley Street, now Standin' on the Corner Park. A mural and a statue of a musician in the park illustrate the song. (Joe Sonderman.)

IMAGES
of America

ROUTE 66 IN ARIZONA

Joe Sonderman

ARCADIA
PUBLISHING

Published by Arcadia Publishing
Charleston, South Carolina

Printed in the United States of America

Library of Congress Control Number: 2010926985

For all general information, please contact Arcadia Publishing:
Telephone 843-853-2070
Fax 843-853-0044
E-mail sales@arcadiapublishing.com
For customer service and orders:
Toll-Free 1-888-313-2665

Visit us on the Internet at www.arcadiapublishing.com

For Lorraine, Cathy, and Kim

CONTENTS

ACKNOWLEDGMENTS

A book on Route 66 would be impossible without the inspiration of Michael Wallis and works by Thomas Arthur Repp, David Wickline, Quinta Scott, and Marshall Trimble. Jim Hinckley and Michael Ward provided invaluable assistance and images, along with Steve Rider and Phillip Gordon. Thank you to Jared Jackson and Mike Litchfield at Arcadia Publishing. Unless otherwise noted, images are from the author's collection.

INTRODUCTION

From the start, this was no ordinary road, because it was blazed by camels. In 1857, Lt. Edward F. Beale surveyed a wagon road from Fort Defiance, New Mexico, to the Colorado River along the 35th Parallel. The expedition brought along 23 camels to test their usefulness in hauling cargo. The camels were turned loose, and their descendants were spotted into the 20th century.

The Atlantic and Pacific Railroad (later the Santa Fe) closely followed Beale's wagon road, spawning the communities of Holbrook, Winslow, Flagstaff, Williams, Ashfork, Seligman, Kingman, and others. The Fred Harvey Company opened Arizona to mass tourism, constructing lavish Harvey Houses that offered Santa Fe Railroad patrons and locals food and accommodations equal to those in the major cities. The Harvey Houses were ready to serve motorists when the automobile age arrived.

In 1909, J. B. Girand was appointed as territorial engineer to lay out four roads connecting each of the 14 Arizona county seats. One of those roads passed through Springerville and St. Johns before picking up the future path of Route 66. Girand's route also dropped south from Kingman through Yucca and Topock to the Colorado River.

By this time, private promoters were laying out routes with fancy names across the nation. Many spent little on maintenance and took travelers miles out of their way past businesses that made contributions. A bewildering array of non-standardized symbols and color codes marked the trails, which often overlapped.

In 1913, an association mapped out the National Old Trails Road through Arizona, following Girand's route with two exceptions. The new route followed the railroad west from Gallup, New Mexico, via Lupton to Holbrook. At Kingman, the Old Trails Highway headed west across the Black Mountains to Oatman, a very important town at the time. Girand's route between Springerville and Holbrook became a branch of the Old Trails Road.

In 1925, the federal government stepped in to ease the confusion, and a committee assigned numbers to the proposed national routes. East-west routes were given even numbers, with the most important routes ending in "0." The north-south routes received odd numbers, with a number ending in "5" denoting the major highways. Cyrus Avery of Tulsa, Oklahoma, led the committee. He made sure the important-sounding "60" was assigned to the highway between Chicago and Los Angeles through his hometown, even though it was not a true east-west transcontinental route.

Kentucky officials were outraged. Gov. William J. Fields wanted 60 for the transcontinental route through his state. After a battle of angry telegrams, it was agreed that the catchy sounding "66" was acceptable for the Los Angeles–to–Chicago highway. Route 66 would follow the National Old Trails Road through Arizona.

The national highway system went into effect on November 11, 1926, and the newly formed Route 66 Association went to work promoting the highway. Association publicity man Lon Scott came up with the idea of a transcontinental footrace. Nearly 300 runners in the Bunion Derby, promoted by the flamboyant C. C. Pyle, left Los Angeles on March 4, 1928, and the media avidly followed. On March 12, the 127 remaining runners were ferried into Arizona, and they crossed into New Mexico on March 22. Just 55 runners made it to New York City. Andy Payne, a half Cherokee from the Route 66 community of Foyil, Oklahoma, took the $25,000 first prize. Pyle lost thousands of dollars because he expected communities to pay for the privilege of hosting the runners and the accompany bizarre sideshow, but several refused. Route 66 reaped the publicity.

During the Great Depression, thousands of Dust Bowl refugees fled west. In *The Grapes of Wrath*, John Steinbeck called 66 "The Mother Road, the road of flight." For many of those living along the highway in Arizona, Route 66 provided an economic lifeline. The last segment of Route 66 to be paved in Arizona was at Crozier Canyon, a 3.9-mile project completed on July 13, 1937. Route 66 was paved from coast to coast by mid-1938.

During World War II, Route 66 was vital for moving troops and equipment to installations such as the Navajo Army Depot at Bellemont. Another great migration took place as people sought defense jobs in California. Rationing of tires and gasoline curtailed recreational traveling. The glory years of Route 66 began when the war ended.

In 1946, Bobby Troup's "Route 66" became a huge hit for Nat King Cole, further romanticizing Route 66. Americans hit the road in record numbers, and all manner of motels, cafés, gas stations, roadside zoos, and trading posts sprang up. Beginning in 1960, the CBS television series *Route 66* added to the allure.

By that time, the popularity of Route 66 was proving to be its downfall. The torturous route through Oatman was bypassed in 1952. The new route returned to Girand's pathway south from Kingman through Yucca and Topock. In 1956, one out of every six traffic deaths in Arizona occurred on "Bloody 66." In 1959, in just one month, 11 people died on a stretch of Route 66 near Peach Springs.

Congress passed the Interstate Highway Act in 1956, authorizing a 41,000-mile system of divided superhighways that would go around the towns where Route 66 was "The Main Street of America."

Interstate 40 was completed around Flagstaff in 1968, between Ashfork and Kingman in 1975, around Winslow in 1979, and past Holbrook in 1981. A bittersweet ceremony on October 13, 1984, marked the opening of Interstate 40 around Williams, the last community on Route 66 to be bypassed. In 1985, Route 66 was officially decertified. But "The Mother Road" didn't die.

Angel Delgadillo, a barber in Seligman, gathered a group of business owners who formed the Route 66 Association of Arizona in February 1987. With Angel as an unofficial spokesman dubbed the "Guardian Angel of Route 66," their efforts sparked a revival that spread along the entire highway. In November 1987, the Arizona Legislature designated Route 66 between Seligman and Kingman as "Historic Route 66," a designation later applied to the entire route in Arizona. Today travelers come from all over the world to experience a time when getting there was half the fun. Adventure waits at the Interstate 40 off-ramp.

One

NEW MEXICO LINE TO THE PETRIFIED FOREST

Motorists crossing the state line from New Mexico into Arizona saw this billboard, touting some of the natural wonders ahead, erected by the Arizona unit of the U.S. Highway 66 Association. Trading posts and curio stores line the highway at Lupton, named for the man who established the first trading post here.

The state line runs right through the Fort Chief Yellowhorse Trading Post, with its fake animals perched on the bluff. Chief Juan Yellowhorse bought Harry "Indian" Miller's trading post at the Cave of the Seven Devils in 1960, and the post is still operated by the chief's family. Billboards for the post said, "We No Scalpum Paleface. Just Scalpum Wallet."

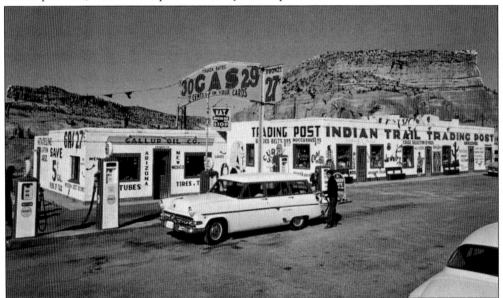

The Ortega family began trading with American Indians in the mid-1800s. Max and Amelia Ortega opened the Indian Trails Trading Post at Lupton on June 21, 1946. Their son, Armand Ortega, is now one of the world's foremost American Indian jewelry dealers. The trading post was demolished to make room for the Interstate 40 service road in 1965.

Claude and Clara Lee owned the Querino Canyon Trading Post and bought Big Arrows from Slim Brazier. When Route 66 was relocated in the 1950s, they abandoned Querino Canyon and built a new Big Arrows. Their daughter Arlene and her husband, Jay Crone, managed it into the late 1960s, offering Arlene's "Squaw Dress Originals."

Corporal Agarn, Sergeant O'Rourke, and the Hekawi Indians never were actually here, but the Fort Courage Trading Post at Houck was based on the 1960s television series *F Troop*. This good old-fashioned tourist trap was originally constructed by the Van de Camps. Later owned by Bill Gipe, J. T. Turner, and Armand Ortega, Fort Courage is now a modern trading post just off the interstate.

Al Berry operated the Log Cabin Trading Post near Sanders, built of pine logs and known for illicit gambling. Berry advertised the "Largest Free Zoo in the Southwest" and charged tourists to see American Indian ruins he had excavated. Only some ruins and a forlorn wishing well remain today west of the Indian Ruins Store operated by Armand Ortega.

The White Elephant bar, lodge and curio store was originally the Chamese Lodge, constructed by Mitchell Dickens and Robert Cassady Jr. There reportedly were illegal slot machines inside. Al Berry bought the lodge after it went bankrupt and later traded the property to Skeet and Maude Eddens. The White Elephant was destroyed by fire.

The Navapache Café was located in Chambers, named for trading post operator Charles Chambers. Other businesses here included the Cedar Point Trading Post and the original Chambers Trading Post, later owned by Alice and Frank Young. They built the Chieftain Motel on Interstate 40 when Chambers was bypassed.

Charley Jacobs built a very successful business because he was one of the few craftsmen who could cut brittle petrified wood for jewelry. To attract even more business, Jacobs invited Navajo families to sell their rugs, jewelry, and other items while living year-round at his "Navajo Village" west of Chambers. His wandering burros also lured tourists.

Harry C. Osborne operated the Painted Desert Point Trading Post, 21 miles east of Holbrook. There were illegal slot machines inside, the take split with the operators of the Chamese Lodge farther east on Route 66. In 1952, the 78-year-old Osborne shot and killed his mentally ill son, Lee, at the trading post. A coroner's jury ruled he acted in self defense. (Phil Gordon.)

Dotch and Alberta Windsor opened the Painted Desert Trading Post in 1942. They divorced in 1950, and Dotch married Joy Nevin. They advertised a 150-pound canary. When disappointed tourists found it was just a burro, Dotch informed them that prospectors called the burro "the canary of the desert." The post was abandoned after Dotch and Joy split up in 1956, and the lonely ruins remain. (Steve Rider.)

Julia Grant Miller was the sister of Harry "Indian" Miller, owner of the infamous Fort Two Guns at Canyon Diablo. Her Painted Desert Park offered a spectacular view of the Painted Desert. Julia battled with Charles "White Mountain" Smith, superintendent of the Petrified Forest, who said her establishment was unsanitary and unsightly. A lion at the zoo once scalped a visitor.

Julia's son, Charley Jacobs, returned to his mother's land in 1953 and constructed a new trading post and tower. It was partly an effort to get the National Park Service to buy the land before Route 66 was relocated. Since the property was within the Petrified Forest National Monument, the NPS was upset by the "eyesore" and bought Charley's land in 1958. The post was destroyed. (National Park Service.)

The Painted Desert is a marvel of strange landscapes. Bands of colored sediments and clay of the Chinle rock formation have been exposed by erosion, and the beautiful palette changes as the sun moves across the sky. In September 1932, Pres. Herbert Hoover made 53,300 acres part of the Petrified Forest National Monument, now Petrified Forest National Park.

The Painted Desert Inn was originally the Stone Tree House, constructed with petrified wood by Herbert D. Lore in 1924 and purchased by the government in 1936. The Civilian Conservation Corps remodeled it into a Pueblo Revival–style structure. The Fred Harvey Company ran the hotel from 1947 until April 16, 1963. Nearly demolished in 1975, it is now a museum and visitors center.

Two

Petrified Forest to Holbrook

Over 200 million years ago, this area was a vast floodplain where stately pine trees grew. Sand and volcanic ash covered the fallen trees, and over the eons, silica replaced the wood. After the area was lifted above sea level, wind and water eroded the sandstone and shale surrounding the petrified logs, leaving them on the surface today.

After the completion of the Santa Fe Railroad, vast amounts of petrified wood were looted to be sold to tourists. That came to an end after December 8, 1906, when Pres. Theodore Roosevelt declared the Petrified Forest a national monument. It became a national park in 1962, the only national park to include a section of Route 66. A member of the Nez Perce tribe is shown here next to a log dubbed "Old Faithful."

Route 66 could be a dangerous highway. On August 24, 1944, the driver of this Red Bluff oil truck and two soldiers burned to death when the truck overturned and exploded east of Holbrook. The soldiers' vehicle had stalled on the other side of the highway when the truck driver pulled out to pass. (Michael Luke.)

Holbrook was the headquarters for the Whiting Brothers chain of gas stations, which once had over 100 locations in the southwest. The company also operated about 15 motels, including two in Holbrook. The Whiting Brothers Motel at 2402 Navajo Boulevard became the Sahara Inn and has a distinctive saw tooth gabled roof.

The 26-unit 66 Motel at 2105 Navajo Boulevard opened in 1948. R. R. Rogers was the owner. It was later owned by Mr. and Mrs. H. S. Harvey. The café became Bob Lyall's 66 Steak House in the 1950s. It then became the Hilltop Café, operated by Ray and Barbara Williams. The 66 Motel and Hilltop Café are still in business today.

At Young's Corral, they said, "A stranger is a friend we haven't met—yet!" Located at 865 Navajo Boulevard, Young's opened in 1948 and is still a popular watering hole today. Murals on the side of the building show a historical view and celebrate the Corral's Route 66 heritage. The unusual sign out front features the tail end of a horse.

Jack Paine originally owned the Pow Wow Trading Post, later purchased by Edward and Pauline Leopold. Their son Ken and his wife, Gwen, took over in 1946. A massive Kachina sign (upper left) now stands in front of the Pow Wow. The wording was changed from "Motel" to "Rocks" when the motel units were converted into the rock shop.

Ken and Gwen Leopold also owned the El Patio Autel across the street from the Pow Wow. Later the El Patio Motel, it was once the home of an intimidating-looking chair made from five and a half sets of elk horns. Gwen's grandfather Edward Leopold made the chair, later moved to the Holbrook Elks Lodge. The motel no longer stands.

The Holbrook Motel at 720 Navajo Boulevard advertised as a new motel in 1958. There were 62 modern units promoted as being away from the railroad noise. The motel boasted "Wall-to-wall carpeting, refrigerated air-conditioning, and individually controlled wall heaters." It became the America's Best Value Inn.

Built in 1898, the old Navajo County Courthouse is now a museum reportedly haunted by the ghost of George Smiley. Smiley was slated to hang for murder on December 8, 1899. But the press got hold of a cheerfully worded invitation to the necktie party issued by Sheriff Frank Wattron. Arizona governor Nathan Oakes Murphy reprimanded Wattron and issued a 30-day stay. Smiley did hang on January 8, 1900, after more subdued invitations were issued.

Looking south on Navajo Boulevard approaching Arizona Street in Holbrook, the Green Lantern Café is at right. Originally located further south, it was operated for many years by Nevert and Gilbert Scorse and was recommended by Jack Rittenhouse in his *Guidebook to Route 66*. This building was occupied by a music store and a shoe store as of 2010.

Holbrook is named for Henry Holbrook, chief engineer for the Atlantic and Pacific Railroad. The view looks north on Navajo Boulevard at West Hopi Drive. Chester B. Campbell's Coffee House opened in 1928 and was known for Son-of-a-Bitch Stew, a cowboy dish made with the heart, liver, brains, and other calf organs.

Dick Mester operated Campbell's Coffee House during World War II and then opened his own place catering to bus passengers on that site. Mester's Automat Cafeteria advertised as the "First eating establishment of this kind in Arizona." The building at the southeast corner of Navajo Boulevard and Hopi Drive still stands.

The Holbrook area is a haven for roadside dinosaurs. These were made by Adam Luna, owner of the Rainbow Rock Shop at 101 Navajo Boulevard. There is a bronze dinosaur sculpture in the city park just a block away, and comical dinosaurs chomp on bloody mannequins at Stewart's Petrified Wood, east of town on Interstate 40.

Joe and Aggie Montano opened their café in 1943. In 1965, they moved to the location shown here at 120 West Hopi Drive. The building had formerly housed the Cactus Café. Their daughter Alice and her husband, Stanley Gallegos, took over in 1978. Today, their children run Joe and Aggie's Café, the oldest restaurant in Holbrook.

The 26-unit Woods Inn at 235 West Hopi Drive opened in 1960 and was later known as Pope's Inn. It is still in operation today as the Holbrook Inn. Motels such as this one thrived much longer than in many Route 66 communities, because Holbrook was not bypassed until 1981. After the interstate opened, 45 businesses closed within a year.

CHIEF
JOE SEKAKUKU
A Hopi
Snake Chief

Chief Joe's Trading Post, which stood at 510 West Hopi Drive, was one of the few actually owned by an American Indian. Joe Sekakuku once worked for the Fred Harvey Company, performing Hopi snake dances for tourists at the Grand Canyon. His original post was at Two Guns, and he was a witness at the murder trail of Harry Miller (see page 52).

Built, owned, and operated by Ed and Mae Burton, the ranch-style Western Motel at 521 West Hopi Drive originally had 21 units, later expanded to 26. The old sign featuring a smiling cowboy was moved to the Butterfield Stage Company Steakhouse next door, and the motel is now a storage business.

The Chief Motel, at 608 West Hopi Drive, was originally the Exclusive Motel. Owned by William Finder, it burned suspiciously in 1975. Finder's Commercial Hotel in Flagstaff was also torched hours after being condemned that same year. A parking lot wall on the Chief site features a big painted map of Route 66 advertising the Butterfield Stage Company Steakhouse across the street.

The Motoraunt Coffee Shop, Dining Room, and "Refined Cocktail Bar" opened on March 27, 1947. It offered arts and crafts by Navajo Indians, and organist Fred Laskowsky was regularly on hand to play requests. The Motoraunt developed into the Butterfield Stage Company Steakhouse in the 1970s, complete with a stagecoach perched on the roof.

The Sea Shell Motel at 612 West Hopi Drive was part of a small chain. There were also Sea Shell Motels in Lordsburg, New Mexico; Blythe, California; Safford, Arizona; and Gila Bend, Arizona. The expanded Sea Shell later became a Whiting Brothers Motor Hotel, then the Golden Door Motor Hotel, and finally the Economy Inn.

In 1938, Chester Lewis saw Frank Redford's Wigwam Village No. 2 at Cave City, Kentucky, and decided to build one of his own. Wigwam Village No. 6 opened on June 1, 1950. Redford was paid the proceeds from pay radios in the rooms in return for use of the plans. Texaco later ordered Lewis to replace the large wigwam in the center with a traditional station.

The Wigwam closed in 1974 and was vacant until 1988. Its future was in doubt after Chester Lewis died in 1986. But the Lewis family restored the 15 steel-framed and stucco-covered wigwams. In this 1954 view, the Forest Motel is visible across Route 66. It was owned by Kale and Beulah Soehner, and a supermarket now occupies the site.

The Sundown Dining Room and Coffee Shop was adjacent to the Sundown Motel, owned by Albert and Jack Ong. Fern Daugherty was also an operator of the 26-unit motel one block west of the Wigwam. The motel and the former restaurant building are still standing as of 2010 along with the big sign, which has been covered with white paint.

In 1956, the Whiting Brothers DeLuxe Motel at 902 West Hopi Drive was expanded to become the Whiting Motor Hotel with the Kolob Restaurant next door. Al and Helene Frycek advertised it as "A new motel designed and furnished for your comfort." There were 57 units with "individually controlled hi-fi music."

The Whiting Motor Hotel became the Sun N' Sand Motel, still operated by Al and Helene Frycek at the time of this view. It closed in 2001. According to the city of Holbrook, owner Robert McIntosh neglected the property. As of 2010, the Sun N' Sand is still standing but is boarded up. The shell of the sign remains.

The Plainsman Restaurant at 1001 West Hopi Drive recalls the days when cowboys of the Aztec Land and Cattle Company, or the "Hashknife Outfit," terrorized Holbrook. There were 26 shooting deaths in 1886, when the population was about 250. The restaurant closed in 2005 but was later renovated by Jon and Carol States.

The Desert View Lodge at 1009 West Hopi Drive was owned and operated by Ruby and Jim McDermott and originally had 23 units. It was later owned by Norm and Adelyne Hormandl. In 1956, an 11-unit second deck was added, and the Desert View Lodge became the first motel in Holbrook with a swimming pool. It became the Star Inn.

These motorists are lined up at the Arizona Department of Agriculture and Horticulture Inspection Station just west of Holbrook. R. P. Harvey served as the chief inspector. In 1946, about 35,000 westbound vehicles passed through the station each month. By July 1959, that number had risen to 100,869.

Three

JOSEPH CITY TO WINSLOW

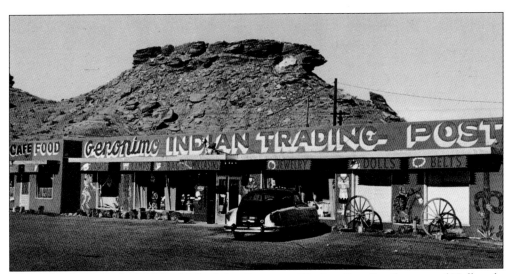

About 1950, "Doc" Hatfield established the Geronimo Trading Post 5 miles west of Holbrook. Carl Kempton took over in 1967. In 1974, he constructed the current Geronimo Indian Store building, which actually has its own exit off Interstate 40. Visitors can see the World's Largest Petrified Log, weighing in at 89,000 pounds.

Otis Baird served as deputy sheriff for Navajo County while he was running his Apache Fort trading post. Inside was a collection of snakes and a pet mountain lion. Otis would drop rattlesnakes into the jewelry cases at night in case of a break in. He sold to Paul Hatch in 1973, and the fort burned down in 1984.

The Hopi Village Indian Store and Café became Howdy Hank's Trading Post. Hank left town under lurid circumstances, selling to V. P. Richards, who later sold to Max Ortega. Ortega renamed it the Sitting Bull Trading Post. It is now the Historic Route 66 Hay Sales and Feed Store. A cartoon Howdy Hank has been repainted on the building.

Mormons settled Joseph City in 1876. Glenn Blansett and his sons built the Pacific Motel in 1947. A gas station was added, and the motel grew to 21 units. Glenn moved to lease the Jack Rabbit Trading Post in 1961, and he bought it in 1967. The station is now Heritage Glass at 4500 Main Street, and the motel units are now a storage business.

Scout, trapper, prospector, and poet Frederick "San Diego" Rawson established San Diego's Old Frontier Trading Post in 1927. He sold in 1947, and the business was awarded to Ella Blackwell in a 1955 divorce settlement. Ella had mental problems, talking to mannequins and claiming the post was established in 1873. Ella's Frontier was abandoned when she died in 1984.

This landmark was originally a Santa Fe Railroad building and then the Arizona Herpetorium. In 1949, Jack Taylor let the snakes loose and opened the Jack Rabbit Trading Post. Glenn Blansett leased it in 1961. Blansett bought it in 1967, as he retired from the state senate. His daughter and son-in-law took over in 1969. They sold the Jack Rabbit to their daughter and son-in-law, Cynthia and Antonio Jaquez, in 1995.

Billboards featuring a black bunny on a yellow background made the Jack Rabbit an icon. Taylor teamed with Wayne Troutner of the Store for Men in Winslow to erect billboards for their businesses as far away as New York. The wooden billboard blaring "here it is" across from the trading post is the 1949 original.

This stone-pillared sign welcomed Route 66 travelers to Winslow. It promoted the Hopi Snake Dance, described as the "most spectacular religious rite in the world." A caravan sponsored by the chamber of commerce left Winslow on the morning of each dance at the Hopi Villages. The altered sign still stands today.

Billed as "Winslow's Newest and Finest" in 1958, the 45-room Knotty Pines Motel, at 1500 East Third Street, had pine paneling in each unit. It was owned by Ralph and Virginia Miller with Ruth and Bill Martin. Note the fierce bear standing guard in front of the Bear Den Cocktail Lounge. P. T.'s Bar occupies this site today.

John B. Drumm came to Winslow to open a barbershop in 1889. He opened his 20-unit auto court two blocks from the center of town in 1937 and ran it until 1944. John served seven terms as justice of the peace. His wife, Frona Parr Drumm, was Winslow's first female insurance agent. The Drumm family also owned a mortuary.

The Desert Sun Motel, at 1000 East Third Street, was constructed in 1953. It advertised 33 "Comfortable and attractive air conditioned units with the finest furnishings. Free radio available and away from railroad noise." As of 2010, the Desert Sun Motel is still in business across from the Falcon Restaurant.

Jim, George, and Pete Kretsedemas emigrated from Greece to join an uncle at the Falcon Restaurant, which opened on July 9, 1955. The brothers would run the restaurant at 1113 West Third Street for the next 43 years. The Falcon, which actor Richard Burton once said had the best food between Hollywood and Kansas, is still in business.

In the 1940s, Lee Elzey built the 16-unit 66 Motor Court for Adam Mace next to Elzey's tire shop at 1102 East Second Street. Elzey had taken the motor court over completely by 1950. He renamed it the L-Z Court. The motel was later expanded to 28 units and became the L-Z Budget Motel. It was still standing but boarded up as of 2010.

The La Siesta Motel No. 2 at 911 East Second Street consisted of 23 units. It was owned by Mr. and Mrs. E. R. Crozier at the time of this view. Other owners included Mr. and Mrs. John Poeth and Mr. and Mrs. Lyle Douglass. Duncan Hines recommended the La Siesta, described by AAA in 1954 as "A pleasing motel with some large family units."

A sign featuring a giant angel welcomed travelers at Gabrielle's Kitchen on Second Street. Owned by Mr. and Mrs. W. H. Hunt, Gabrielle's advertised "Good Home Cooking" along with "Real Home Made Pies" and the "Best Coffee on Hi-Way No. 66." It was known as Gabrielle's Pancake House during the 1960s and 1970s, and the building now houses a Chinese restaurant. (Mike Ward.)

BEACON MOTEL
HIGHWAY 66, WINSLOW, ARIZ.

42860

In 1957, AAA described the 10-unit Motel Beacon, at 600 East Second Street, as "a modest motel." Their motto was "Comfort for you." This card noted that the Beacon had "ten air conditioned units, tile baths, carpeted floors, easy chairs, reading lights and first class beds." The Beacon was later expanded to 14 units and painted lime green. The site is now occupied by a storage business and auto service firm.

The Marble Motel, at 512 East Third Street, was built in the 1940s. The motel was remodeled and a new facade was added in 1952. It is now Earl's Motor Court, operated by Lee and Floranel Earl. They advertise "sleeping on the corner in Winslow, Arizona" at the oldest Route 66 motel still operating in Winslow.

La Posada was the last of the great Fred Harvey hotels to be constructed, opening in 1930 and designed by Mary Colter. The Harvey Restaurant closed in 1956, and the hotel closed on January 15, 1959. Gutted and used as offices by the Santa Fe, it was nearly torn down. Allan Affeldt and his wife, Tina Mion, began restoration in 1997.

This view looks west on Second Street approaching Kinsley Street. Standin' on the Corner Park now occupies the site of Winslow Drugs and J.C. Penney on the far left. The park features a two-story mural by John Pugh and a life-size sculpture of a musician by Ron Adamson illustrating the Eagles song "Take It Easy." The mural was saved when the old J.C. Penney building burned on October 18, 2004.

Wayne Lowell Troutner established a dry cleaning plant in 1942, delivering laundry to other towns by plane. He later moved the cleaners to the back and opened a western wear store, the Store for Men. Charley Holmes designed the curvaceous cowgirl that adorned the sign and hundreds of billboards. Troutner sold in 1990, and the building later burned. (Old Trails Museum.)

Route 66 originally followed Second Street, past the Star Court, which later became the Starlite Motel. In 1951, Second Street became one-way eastbound, and westbound traffic was shifted to Third Street, making Winslow the first community in Arizona to establish one-way highway traffic. Interstate 40 bypassing Winslow opened on October 9, 1979.

Grover Cleveland Bazell was a lawyer and newspaper owner who opened a garage and a Buick dealership in 1921. The cabins at the Bazell Modern Camp were later connected, and it became the Bazell Modern Court, operated by Mr. and Mrs. Robert Powell. Some of the structures still stand and are used as private residences.

The Entré Restaurant and Cocktail Lounge opened in 1958 and is still in business today at 1919 West Second Street. It was operated by Steve and Helen Sponduris, who were married in a big Greek wedding at the restaurant in 1961. In 1962, the Entré opened the Carnival Room, advertising Winslow's first *Bierstube* (beer hall).

Four

METEOR CITY TO WINONA

Former Hawaiian bandleader Ray Meany and his wife, Ella Blackwell, owned the Hopi House at Route 66 and Arizona Route 99, known as Leupp Corner. They also owned the Old Frontier in Joseph City. When they divorced, Ella got the Old Frontier and Ray swapped the Hopi House for a motel in California. Interstate 40 doomed the Hopi House.

Winslow was promoted as "Meteor City," and Joseph Sharber took the name for his service station, constructed in 1938. Jack Newsum took over the station in 1941, opened a trading post, and erected a sign on Route 66 reading "Meteor City—Population 1." Jack is shown here with his wife, Gloria, having changed the sign to read "Population 2" after they were married in 1946. (Old Trails Museum.)

Jack and Gloria Newsum are posed in front of the original Meteor City Trading Post. Jack died in 1960, and Gloria became known as "The Witch of Route 66" for handing down harsh speeding fines as justice of the peace. This building burned in the 1960s. Since 1979, the trading post has been housed in a geodesic dome. (Old Trails Museum.)

Meteor City was featured in the 1984 film *Starman*, starring Jeff Bridges. A new dome was erected after a fire in 1990. Dan and Judi Kempton took over in 1989 but closed down in 2001. In 2002, Richard and Emelia Benton revived Meteor City. The post is home to the world's longest map of Route 66, restored in 2003. (Library of Congress.)

Hopi Indians believed this massive crater was caused by a god who was cast from heaven. It was discovered by the white man in 1871 and at the time was believed to have been of volcanic origin. Meteor Crater is 4,150 feet across, 3 miles around the top, and 570 feet deep. The rim rises more than 150 feet above the surrounding desert.

OLD METEOR MINE AND GHOST TOWN
SOUTH RIM OF METEOR CRATER ON
U.S. 66 AT METEOR ARIZONA

Philadelphia mining engineer Daniel Moureau Barringer set up mining equipment at the crater in 1903. Barringer was ridiculed when he said the crater was caused by a meteor. He spent the rest of his life and much of his private capital searching for the meteor, finding only fragments. Barringer's theory was accepted after he died in 1929.

Harry Locke was interested in Dr. Barringer's work and owned the land where Route 66 met the road to the crater. Harry and his wife, Hope, operated a service station at the spot they called Meteor Junction. Locke became well known for cartoon postcards such as this one, all the while dreaming of building a meteor museum.

To raise money for their dream, the Lockes leased Meteor Station to the colorful "Rimmy Jim" Giddings (at right) in August 1933. Giddings erected signs saying he kept a graveyard for salesmen and placed an intercom beneath the outhouse seats to startle unsuspecting travelers. Giddings died in 1943. Ruth and Sid Griffin would run Rimmy Jim's until Interstate 40 came through.

Harry Locke's Meteor Crater Observatory opened in the late 1930s but failed to make money and was lost to foreclosure. Locke developed a comic strip called *Desert Cuties* and was gaining acclaim when he agreed to help out the short-handed Winslow Police Department. He died at age 56 after battling a drunk prisoner. Dr. Harvey Nininger took over the observatory, opening the American Meteorite Museum on October 19, 1946.

Dr. Harvey Nininger's American Meteorite Museum attracted 33,000 visitors in the first year and became a renowned center for research. It housed about 5,000 meteorites, the largest collection of any institution at the time. But Route 66 was moved to the north in 1949, and museum closed in 1953. The crumbling ruins remain today.

A town "wilder than Tombstone" sprouted when construction of the Atlantic and Pacific Railroad was halted at Canyon Diablo due to financial difficulties in 1881–1882. Canyon Diablo's Hell Street was lined with 14 saloons, 10 gambling dens, and 4 brothels. The first marshal was killed five hours after being sworn in, and only one lawman survived as long as 30 days. The town died when this bridge was finished. (National Archives.)

Earl Cundiff's Canyon Lodge store and camp opened in 1924 at the National Old Trails Road Bridge over Canyon Diablo. In March 1925, he leased it to the mystical Harry "Indian" Miller. Miller had lived among the Philippine headhunters and worked in silent films. Billing himself as "Chief Crazy Thunder," he built a roadside zoo and named the complex Fort Two Guns after a film starring his pal William S. Hart.

In 1878, Navajos trapped 42 murderous Apaches in a cave near Canyon Diablo, filled the entrance with brush, and set it on fire. The Apaches died horribly. Harry Miller built fake ruins and made the "Apache Death Cave" part of his roadside attraction. In 1926, Miller shot and killed his landlord, Earl Marion Cundiff. Cundiff was unarmed, but Miller claimed self-defense and was acquitted. (Phil Gordon.)

This view shows the roadside zoo at Two Guns. Harry Miller was never forgiven by some locals for shooting Earl Cundiff. Miller was also convicted of defacing Cundiff's tombstone, which read "Killed by Indian Miller." Facing more legal troubles, Miller left in 1930 to open another business at the Cave of the Seven Devils, on Route 66 at the New Mexico–Arizona state line.

Louise Cundiff, Earl's widow, married Phillip Hesch in 1934. Route 66 was relocated in 1938, and Hesch constructed this store, station, and residence. He reestablished the zoo behind the store. Benjamin Dreher built a modern motel and station at Two Guns in 1963 that burned spectacularly in 1971. Only ghostly ruins remain at Two Guns today.

The Toonerville Trading Post was one of six trading posts on Route 66 between Winslow and Winona. Earl Tinnin ran the businesses at Two Guns from 1933 to 1935 before opening Toonerville. He sold in 1954. Owner Daniel "Slick" McAlister was killed in a robbery here on August 30, 1971. The building was converted to a private home and still stands. (Phil Gordon.)

The Canyon Padre Trading Post became the Twin Arrows Trading Post in 1954. Jean and William Troxell ran it from 1955 to 1985. Two giant arrows made from utility poles out front made Twin Arrows famous. It closed in the late 1990s, but the arrows have been restored. The Hopi tribe plans to renovate the buildings for an "Indian Marketplace."

Winona is not really a town but gets a mention in the song "(Get Your Kicks on) Route 66" because it rhymes with Arizona. It actually lies 18 miles east of Flagstaff and is listed out of sequence in the song. Billy Adams built the Winona Trading Post in 1924, and his wife, Myrtle, became the state's first female postmaster. Adams added a 14-unit motel in 1925 and built a new trading post when Route 66 was realigned in the 1950s.

Five

FLAGSTAFF

Gibson's "Chix Fry" (C H I X)
3 miles East of Flagstaff, Arizona
On U. S. Highway '66' and '89'

GIBSON'S
CHIX FRY
FRIED CHICKEN

Ira, Helen, and Jerry Gibson opened Gibson's Chix Fry east of Flagstaff in 1945 offering "one-half unjointed fried chicken, shoe string potatoes, and bread in a wax lined box." The Gibsons invited patrons to "visit our Broiler Plant and Butcher Shop." It became Kenney's Chix Fry in 1960 and was in business into the mid-1960s.

W. W. and Lucretia Sample opened Camp Elden in 1934. W. W. Sample and his brother started the Red Bluff gas station chain, which grew to include locations across Arizona on Route 66. Lucretia Sample would not allow liquor to be sold, but a liquor store opened here after they sold in 1945. Note that gas was selling for 19¢ per gallon. (Michael Luke.)

Starlite Lanes at 3406 East Santa Fe Avenue opened on November 9, 1957. They advertised "16 lanes, AMF Automatic Pinspotters, AMF Tele-Scores, underground ball returns, luxurious cocktail lounge and a free baby sitting room with a capable attendant on duty." Starlite Lanes is still in business today.

Taxidermist and sportsman Dean Eldredge built a log cabin around five huge ponderosa pines to display his collection of 30,000 mounts and oddities. "The Zoo," as it was known by locals, opened on June 20, 1931. Doc Williams turned it into a nightclub in 1936, after Eldredge died and the collection was sold off. Don Scott, who played with Bob Wills and the Texas Playboys, made the old museum a country music showcase in the 1960s.

Don Scott's wife, Thorna, died after falling down the stairs at the Museum Club in 1973. Shattered, Don took his own life two years later. Their ghosts are said to haunt the club. Martin and Stacie Zanzucchi ran the Museum Club from 1978 until 2005. Now operated by Joe and Shannyn Lange, the club is one of the best-known roadhouses on Route 66.

Phillip Johnston saved an untold number of lives during World War II. Raised among the Navajos, he developed a code based on their complex, unwritten language. The Navajo "Code Talkers" served in every Marine assault in the Pacific from 1942 to 1945. E. B. Goble built El Pueblo Motel for Johnston in 1936. It still stands today.

Seven motels were constructed in Flagstaff during 1963, including the Pony Soldier Motel at 3030 East Santa Fe Avenue. The 90-unit Pony Soldier advertised the "Largest Pool in Northern Arizona." It was operated by Paul Greer until 1977 and then by Doris and Joseph Childers. The motel is now the Best Western Pony Soldier Inn and Suites.

Joe and Lila Lockhard, her sons Howard and Bob Leonard, and Bob's wife, Norma, bought a motel, station, and Trixie's Diner in 1942. They named the motel the L and L and planned to call the café the Let's Eat. But Bob's uncle said it needed a zippier name. Miz Zip's, with "Let's Eat" in neon on the facade, is still serving locals and travelers.

Myron Wells, owner of the 66 Motel, served two terms as president of the Arizona chapter of the Route 66 Association. He led the No By-Pass Committee, a group that fought the Interstate 40 bypass and then tried to ban any new businesses on I-40 or between Route 66 and the new highway. The 66 Motel survived and is still in business today at 2100 East Santa Fe Avenue. (Mike Ward.)

ARROWHEAD LODGE - U. S. 66 and 89 - Flagstaff, Ariz. RECOMMENDED BY

Rex E. Goble's Auto Court at 2010 East Santa Fe Avenue became the Arrowhead Lodge after he died in 1941. In June 1959, it was remodeled into the Gaslite Motel, "With a friendly 'glow' that's difficult to leave—impossible to forget." In the 1960s, the name changed to the Twilite Motel. It is now the Arrowhead Lodge and Apartments.

"Gateway to Grand Canyon"
U.S. HIGHWAYS 66 & 89 . . .   East Entrance   . . . FLAGSTAFF, ARIZONA

Advertised as the "Motel with the VIEW," the Wonderland Motel opened at 2000 East Santa Fe Avenue in 1956. Owners Waldo and Adelyne Spelta advertised the 20-unit motel as "Flagstaff's Newest and Finest," with "Nature's air conditioning." It is still in business and appears to be in great shape.

Mr. and Mrs. Lester Smith opened the Frontier Motel at 1700 East Santa Fe Avenue on September 8, 1956. It originally had 26 units, later expanded to 31. It was later operated by Don Toalston, and then George and Vera Skylstead operated it from 1957 into the 1970s. The Frontier was demolished in 2008.

Harold Melville built the Western Hills Motel at 1580 East Santa Fe Avenue in 1953. Charles O. Greening owned it from 1954 to 1969. The impressive animated neon sign is the oldest in Flagstaff. A string of Thai establishments later occupied the restaurant, and Craig Chang opened the Pho Dai Loc Vietnamese Restaurant here in 2008.

Mr. and Mrs. Jack McCorhan opened the Skyline Motel on May 14, 1948, at 1526 East Santa Fe Avenue. Later owners included Mr. and Mrs. Fred G. Long, Lester Smith and his wife, and C. D. Samuel and Stan North. The Skyline originally had 22 units, later expanded to 28. It became the Red Rose Inn Motel, still in business today.

Earl Tinnin, who had constructed the Toonerville Trading Post, owned the Ben Franklin Motel at 1416 East Santa Fe Avenue. It was later owned by Mr. and Mrs. Ray Young. Ernest Castro, a Flagstaff public school teacher, and his wife, Vera, operated it from 1961 until 1976. Later the West Wind Motel, the site is now a shopping center.

This restaurant at 914 East Santa Fe Avenue was simply named the Steak House, operated for many years by Maurice and Mary Grant. It was the Pharaoh Restaurant in the 1960s and later became the Steak House again. This postcard advertises "Complete One-Stop Car Service While You Eat." The Norvel Owens Mortuary stands here today.

There were 17 "modern, clean comfortable and convenient units with private garages" and a Mobil station at the Flagstaff Motor Village, 402 East Santa Fe Avenue. Gordon and Jane Beckley ran the motel for the Babbitt family from 1949 to 1969. The station was closed in 1959, and the motel site is now the Jim Babbitt Ford used car lot.

On July 4, 1876, a group of immigrants cut the limbs off a pine tree for a flag staff to celebrate the U.S. centennial. A railroad camp established in April 1880 was named Flag Staff, shortened to one word in 1881. Before construction of a railroad overpass in 1934, Route 66 turned onto Beaver Street to Phoenix Avenue and Mike's Pike.

The railroad camp was relocated a bit to the east in 1883, and "New Town" sprang up. Railroad Avenue, the future Route 66, is in the foreground in this view of New Town. At right is the Brannen General Store, the first stone building. James Vail's saloon is on the left. Between the structures is present-day San Francisco Street. (Library of Congress.)

An old boxcar served as the depot when the railroad arrived in Flagstaff on August 1, 1882. It grew to four boxcars before a stone depot was built in 1889. The Santa Fe completed a new depot just to the west in 1926. Now the Flagstaff Visitor's Center, it is of English Tudor design, with a steeply pitched roof to shed the heavy snow. (Mike Ward.)

Eddie Wong opened the Grand Canyon Café at 110 East Santa Fe Avenue in 1938. His brother Albert joined him in 1940. A 1950 expansion added the distinctive brick front, windows rounded on one side, and stainless steel canopy over the entrance. The Grand Canyon Café is still in business today, noted for its chicken fried steak.

Looking west on Santa Fe Avenue, a sign on the Vail Building points toward Edwin D. Babbitt's Ford dealership. The Commercial Hotel opened in 1888. It had the first indoor plumbing in town and was the headquarters of Western novelist Zane Grey. An arsonist destroyed the landmark on November 14, 1975, just hours after it was condemned.

The same view in 1948 shows Black's Lounge in the Vail Building, later Club 66. Jerry Midgley's Rose Tree Café was operated by Wong June Jr. into the 1950s. J. R. Cooper's Buffett replaced Joe Bender's Café. Lee Jenkins ran Wigwam Indian Curios, and Jerry Andreatos owned the El Patio Café, now the Flagstaff Brewing Company.

Photographer Frank Sofea turned to the restaurant business in 1922 when his eyesight failed. He moved his Black Cat Café to 6 East Santa Fe Avenue in the early 1930s. It later became the Out West Café. Wing Sing Gee took over in 1961 and opened the Hong Kong Restaurant. The building now houses a sushi bar.

Khatter Joseph Nackard built the Downtowner Auto Court in 1929 on the site of an old brothel on San Francisco Street. In 1933, the cabins were connected to form the Nackard Inn. Nackard ran an illegal slot machine operation, paying part of the proceeds to the chamber of commerce. The inn became the Downtowner Motel in the 1950 and is now apartments.

Albert N. Du Beau's motel was the first in Arizona to offer amenities for motorists such as garages, sheets, and steam heat. It opened at 19 West Phoenix Street, a block off Route 66, in 1929. There were 28 units with his residence and office in front. It is now the Du Beau International Hostel. Albert's daughter Clara once ran the Black Cat Café.

Salvador Esparza was a carpenter who used sandstone and fieldstone to construct his Sierra Vista Motel, which opened on May 19, 1948, at 9 East Phoenix Avenue. There were 21 units decorated in Spanish Colonial style. The large neon sign atop the Sierra Vista remained in place until a new roof was added around 2007–2008.

John Weatherford's Hotel at Aspen Avenue and Leroux Street opened on January 1, 1900. Weatherford also built the Majestic Opera House, which collapsed under 6 feet of snow on December 31, 1915. Its replacement, the Orpheum, is visible in the background. Henry Taylor and his wife, Sam, have restored the historical hotel.

City leaders held a public subscription to build a new hotel downtown that opened on January 1, 1927. A 12-year-old girl won the contest to name the hotel when she suggested Monte Vista, Spanish for "mountain view." The hotel was publicly owned until the early 1960s. The Monte Vista is the oldest continuously operating hotel in Flagstaff.

Arthur Vandevier spent 13 years enforcing the law in Coconino County, opening the Vandevier Lodge with his wife, Laura, in June 1941. It was expanded into a motel in 1953 with seven additional units and a new sign. The motel, at 402 West Santa Fe Avenue, was torn down in May 1977, and apartments were constructed on the site.

Joe L. Sharber and Haydee Lane opened the Lane Motel on February 26, 1948, at 122 West Santa Fe Avenue. In 1958, the Lanes sold the motel to Diamond Sampson, who also owned the Snow Bowl Motel. Sampson tore down the gas station. It later became the Townhouse Motel, now the Rodeway Inn Downtown.

The L Motel was operated by Mr. and Mrs. Luther L. Jones and later by Mr. and Mrs. Alvin Arntsen. In 1954, AAA described the motel as "nicely furnished" with 13 open garages. The L Motel at 121 South Sitgreaves Street (now South Milton Road) originally had 15 units, later expanded to 20, and developed into the Rodeway Inn University.

The Lumber Jack Café opened in 1961. It was originally Tony Souris's Steakhouse, which opened in 1946. Robert and Violet Morrison sold the Lumber Jack to Martin, Hank, and Matt Zanzucchi in 1974, and it became Granny's Closet Restaurant. The café's two giant lumberjacks now guard the Walkup Skydome at Northern Arizona University.

The Spur Motel, at 224 Mike's Pike, opened in 1956. It was operated by Mr. and Mrs. Chester Dohr and later by Mr. and Mrs. R. E. Leaders. In 1957, AAA described the 15-unit motel at the entrance to the university as "a very nice new motel with attractively furnished one and two room units." It is now the Knight's Inn.

Lemuel and Milton Stroud founded the small Park Plaza Motel chain, with locations on Route 66 at Flagstaff, Amarillo, Tulsa, and St. Louis. Lemuel Stroud built units in the back that served as motel rooms in the summer and as the Stroud Hall dormitory when Arizona State College, now Northern Arizona University, was in session.

The Golden Drumstick opened in 1952 next to the Park Plaza Motel. The restaurant offered a dinner of chicken, fries, and honey for $1. There were also Golden Drumstick locations in Phoenix and Tucson. George Nackard opened the Gables Restaurant and Cameo Room here on June 5, 1959. The Gables was once home to KEOS radio, and the building is now the Mandarin Supper Buffet.

This view looks west at the intersection of Route 66 and U.S. 89A. Phoenix developer Andy Womack's "Spanish western frontier style" El Rancho Motel (right) opened on December 9, 1947, and became the Flamingo Motel in 1959. It closed in 1986 and was demolished in 1997. A Barnes and Noble bookstore now occupies the site.

In 1954, Flamingo Hotels bought the El Rancho and constructed the Flamingo Motor Hotel adjoining to the west. In 1959, the Flamingo became the very first Ramada Inn. The name is Spanish for a "shady resting place," according to the company Web site. The motel at 602 West Highway 66 is now a Super Eight.

This marker stood where U.S. 89A split off from Route 66 and 89 at the west end of Flagstaff. Alternate Route 89 takes travelers to scenic Oak Creek Canyon, while Routes 66 and 89 head towards Williams. In 1992, the City of Flagstaff changed the names of parts of Santa Fe Avenue, Sitgreaves Street, and Milton Road back to Route 66.

A lumber mill had served as a landmark at the southwest entrance to Flagstaff since at least 1889. The Saginaw and Manistee Lumber Company operated this mill from 1941 until it was sold and closed down in 1954. A fire set as a high school graduation prank destroyed the landmark on May 29, 1961.

The Saga Motel at 820 West Highway 66 opened in August 1961 and was operated by Barbara and Ray Larkey. The 29-unit motel was later owned by Edward J. Canepa, a Flagstaff civic leader who died in 1973. It is now the Saga Budget Host Inn, and the beautiful blinking blue neon name on the facade remains.

Mr. and Mrs. Jack McCorhan also owned the 29-unit Branding Iron Motel and Dining Room at 1121 West Highway 66. It advertised "Rest away from R.R. Noise" and "Unsurpassed Motel accommodations and fine eating. You'll enjoy the friendly western hospitality and the wonderful mountain air." The site is now a car lot.

The San Francisco Peaks are sacred to many American Indian tribes. The Hopi believed they were the home of the Kachina spirits. There are six peaks, Agassiz, Aubineau, Doyle, Fremont, Humphreys, and Rees. Humphreys Peak is the highest point in Arizona at 12,633 feet. It was named for the general in charge of the early surveyor data. (Mike Ward.)

Six

PARKS TO WILLIAMS

In November 1921, Art Anderson and Don McMillan's store and station opened where the National Old Trails Highway met the road to the Grand Canyon. It is now the Parks in the Pines General Store. The transcontinental Bunion Derby runners passed the store in March 1928. The eventual winner, Andy Payne, is at left. (Kaibab Forest Service.)

Most visitors to the Grand Canyon originally traveled by rail. The first bumpy automobile road from Flagstaff to the canyon opened in 1900. The National Park Service began construction on a good highway in 1928, and it was paved within a few years. This view shows the turn-off from Route 66 between Flagstaff and Williams.

The McHat Inn, located 8 miles east of Williams, became the Wagon Wheel Lodge, operated by Gordon and Juanita McDowell from 1936 to 1959. McDowell was a respected businessman and served on the Coconino County Board of Supervisors. But with the Elmo Dance Hall across the road, the lodge gained a reputation as a brothel during the 1940s. The log building still stands and is now a private residence.

KAIBAB MOTOR LODGE
WILLIAMS, ARIZONA

Mr. and Mrs. Lee Treece ran the 18-unit Kaibab Motor Lodge, 100 yards off Route 66 and "Away from Traffic Noise." It later became the Canyon Motel, which Kevin and Shirley Young converted into the Canyon Hotel and RV Park. Travelers today can sleep in a 1929 Santa Fe Railroad caboose or one of the restored flagstone motel units.

Originally Route 66 made sharp turns and crossed the railroad at grade entering Williams, where Hubert Clark first operated his camp. He built the Grand Canyon Court and Station when an underpass was built in 1932. Clark was a booster of aviation, and the local airport was named in his honor in 1992. Later operated by Harvey Gibbs, the 42 cabins in the pines were demolished in the 1950s for the Thunderbird Inn.

The Thunderbird Inn at 642 East Bill Williams Avenue opened in 1957 and advertised as "The most complete stop on Route 66." It offered 96 luxurious rooms, with a swimming pool, gift shop, restaurant, and cocktail lounge. The Thunderbird became the Mountainside Inn and Conference Center.

In 1958, AAA recommended the new 18-unit El Rancho Motel as "very attractive and well maintained." It advertised "Tubs and Showers in Every Room" and was "Beautifully Furnished." Two more units were later added to the two-story brick motel. The El Rancho is still in business at 617 East Bill Williams Avenue.

C. C. Cheshire ran an auto dealership on West Santa Fe Avenue at Sitgreaves Street in Flagstaff. His brother-in-law A. T. Davis Jr. operated this Cheshire Motors location in Williams at 520 East Bill Williams Avenue. This structure is now occupied by Import Auto Service, but the "Chevrolet" and "Buick" lettering on the smokestack is still visible.

Mr. and Mrs. Lee Treece operated the El Coronado Motel. It originally had 27 rooms, expanded to 42 by the time this view was taken. Located across from Rod's Famous Steak House, the El Coronado offered special day rates for tourists planning to drive across the desert at night. It is now the EconoLodge.

Williams Motel

"The Gateway to Grand Canyon"
U.S. 66 - 89. Williams. Arizona

Dorothy and Dick Boyack's Williams Motel was located next door to Rod's Steak House. It originally consisted of 16 units. An additional structure was later added, bringing the total to 28. Wild West Junction, home of the largest collection of John Wayne memorabilia outside the Wayne family, now occupies this site.

Rodney Graves organized the city's first rodeo and was one of the founders of the Bill Williams Mountain Men. Rod's Steak House opened on August 23, 1946. Graves retired in 1967. In 1985, Stella and Lawrence Sanchez took over the landmark. The sign features Domino the cow, and the souvenir menus are shaped like Domino.

U.S. HIGHWAYS 66 & 89 . . . In Center Of . . . WILLIAMS, ARIZONA

The Del Sue Motel was originally a "Traveler's Tent Camp" in the 1920s. The motel was the first in Williams and opened in 1936. Sue Delaney operated the Del Sue, which is now the Grand Motel. The recently refurbished motel at 234 East Bill Williams Avenue is listed on the National Register of Historic Places.

Roy and Grace Gamble invited travelers to "Enjoy a Night of Rest among the Pines" at the Gateway Motel. They advertised "clean units, all modern, four good restaurants within one-half block." Constructed in 1936, it is now an office plaza, and the former office is now J. D.'s Espresso. Fortunately the sign was preserved.

Everett and Laverne Coffee owned the Mount Williams Motor Court and expanded it into the 16-unit Downtowner Motel. When Route 66 through Williams was divided, part of the back row of units was removed for a driveway to the westbound lanes. It is now the Rodeway Inn and Suites Downtowner Motel at 201 East Bill Williams Avenue.

The Sun Dial Motel at 200 East Bill Williams Avenue was owned by J. H. Venable and later operated by Doc and Bea Starkey. It advertised "nicely furnished, fully carpeted units with tubs and showers, in the tall pine country of Northern Arizona." Renovated in 2003, it is now known as The Lodge.

Originally Bethel's Tourist Court, Starky's Motel was notable for the angled buttresses protruding from the front. Mike "Starky" Starkovich advertised "Ten attractively furnished units." The buttresses are gone, but the motel still stands. It is now the Royal American Inn, at 134 East Bill Williams Avenue.

Hull's Motel Inn was operated by Mr. and Mrs. D. A. Hosack. John and Myrtle Smart bought the 12-cottage motel in the 1940s. The cottages were connected to form 17 units with enclosed garages, and it became Hull's Motel. John died in 1947, and Myrtle ran it until 1958. The motel at 128 Bill Williams Avenue is now the Historic Route 66 Inn.

The Coffee Pot Café (at left) was operated by Mr. and Mrs. John Mills and later by Mr. and Mrs. J. W. Duffield. They advertised "The Best Coffee in Town." The souvenir menus were printed in the shape of a coffee pot. This building now houses the Native America Shop at 117 East Bill Williams Avenue.

On September 17, 1901, Williams became the "Gateway to the Grand Canyon," when the Santa Fe Railroad began service to the natural wonder. The Fray Marcos de Niza Hotel was completed in 1908. The Fred Harvey Company ran the restaurant. The ticket office closed in 1954. In 1989, the Grand Canyon Railway restored the structure to serve as the depot for its steam train excursions to the canyon.

In 1955, Route 66 was divided through Williams. Bill Williams Avenue carried eastbound Route 66, and westbound traffic used Railroad Avenue. Williams was the last community on Route 66 to be bypassed. Bobby Troup sang his "(Get Your Kicks On) Route 66" during the bittersweet ceremony when Interstate 40 opened on October 13, 1984.

August Tetzlaff built this saloon, tailor shop, and bordello on "Whiskey Row" across from the depot in 1897. It was later owned by Longino Moro, who married five times and had 25 children. He is second from left in this view, next to the house madam toting a pistol. The brothel and saloon closed after a murder in the 1940s. Restored by John Holst, the building now houses the Red Garter Bed and Breakfast. (John Holst.)

The Pollock Building, at left, originally had one story and was built with volcanic rock in 1901. Jewell Vaughn and her husband, Reese, operated Vaughn's Indian Store here from 1937 to 1941. They sold to Bernice Montgomery in 1941, and she married Frank Irwin in 1953. The Irwins sold the business to Melvin and Madene Beddo in 1962. The store was moved to a more modern one-story location, shown on page 86.

This view looks east on Bill Williams Avenue from Fourth Street. The original location of Mill's Café housed *Route 66 Magazine* from 1997 to 2001 and is now the Java Cycle Coffee House. In 1908, the pioneering Babbitt brothers of Flagstaff opened a general store with Gus and F. O. Polson. It grew into Babbitt's Department Store, at right.

By the 1950s, Bill Lee's Café occupied the original Mill's Café location. The Mill's had moved to the old Arnold's Café site in the Pollock Building. Sutton's Court, at right, was later a Whiting Brothers Motel and is now the Arizona 9 Motor Hotel. The Sultana Theatre is also on the right. It opened in 1912, originally showing silent movies.

Williams was founded in 1876 and named for William Sherley Williams, a famous trapper and scout of the Santa Fe Trail. The Bill Williams Mountain Men, shown here on parade through town, were founded in 1953 to honor the pioneer trappers and traders. They ride to Phoenix on horseback each year to teach youths about history and have participated in several presidential inaugural parades.

The Westerner Motel, at 530 West Bill Williams Avenue, was owned and managed by Mr. and Mrs. Ray Stewart and later by Melvin and Madene Beddo. The 10-unit motel advertised "Gyramatic Mattresses" and was described by AAA as "a pleasant motel." The Westerner is still in business today.

The rooms were "Air Conditioned by Nature," and they offered "separate dressing rooms" at the 12-unit Highlander Motel. Owners included Marshall and Ruth Ann Duncan as well as Marion and "Whitey" Christensen. The refurbished motel at 533 West Route 66 now advertises, "We may be small, but we will do our best to make you smile."

In 1946, Rodney Graves, who also ran Rod's Steak House, opened Old Smoky's Pancake House and Restaurant, constructed with flat stone very similar to the "giraffe rock" used in the Missouri Ozarks. Mr. and Mrs. Miles Cureton took over in 1952. Elvis Presley once ate here, and Old Smoky's is little changed today.

Norris and Harold Hanson's firm constructed the Norris Motel at 1001 West Highway 66. Opened in 1953, it advertised 16 "distinctively designed units." The Norris was operated by Marion and Reese Morgan, then by L. M. Thompson and George Wyatt, and later by Vern and Fran Thompson. It is now the Best Value Inn.

Harvey J. Gibbs, former owner of Grand Canyon Camp, opened Harvey's Hacienda at the west end of Williams. Max and Pauline Andrews were running it when this view was made. The complex included a 38-unit motel, a coffee shop, a dining room, a curio shop, and a cocktail lounge. The trophies awarded to the Bill Williams Mountain Men were displayed here. The Hacienda no longer stands.

Ashfork Hill, west of Williams, is one of the steepest sections on all of Route 66. Westbound motorists drop about 1,700 feet over 7 miles. The original highway, with its twists and blind crests, was a terror for tourists and truckers alike, especially when traffic increased after World War II. The final section of new highway taming the hill opened in July 1954.

Seven

ASHFORK TO KINGMAN

In 1928, Ezell and Zelma Nelson opened the Copper State Modern Cottages in Ashfork, later the Copper State Court. Ezell built 12 cottages of cobblestone with walls 18 inches thick. The garages had railings inside for tying up horses. The Nelsons operated the Copper State Court until 1975. George and Brenda Bannister bought it in 1989.

The first Harvey House in Ashfork was a wooden structure that burned in 1905. It was replaced by the beautifully landscaped and luxurious Escalante, named after explorer Silvestre Escalante. The hotel closed in 1951, and the restaurant closed in 1953. Local citizens tried to save it, but the landmark was torn down in 1968.

Looking west, Frank Gum's Buffett, the White House Hotel, Arizona Hotel, and 66 Café are at left. At right are McMahan's Texaco, O'Brien's Shamrock Café, Gorra's Pool Hall and Bar, and Joe Gang's Arizona Café and Bar. The Arizona Café building is one of the few structures remaining from the glory days of Route 66, and it is now a church.

Ashfork was a busy place before the Santa Fe Railroad moved the mainline away in 1950. The opening of Interstate 40 in 1979 was another devastating blow. A fire on November 20, 1977, and another on October 7, 1987, virtually wiped out the business district. The quiet town today boasts of being the "Flagstone Capital of the World." (Mike Ward.)

The Hi-Line Modern Auto Court, "Your Home Away From Home," opened in 1936 and was owned by Alton McAbee. It was later owned and operated by Mr. and Mrs. J. R. Edwards. It became the Hi-Line Motel in the 1950s. At that time, a Shell station in the center of the complex was converted to the office and residence.

Joe and Edie DeSoto turned an old Texaco station into DeSoto's Beauty and Barbershop. A 1960 Chrysler DeSoto with "Elvis" at the wheel is perched on the roof. During the glory years of Route 66, the Green Door Bar was located in the building at left, now the Route 66 Grill. It was also known for a time as the Crow Bar. (Library of Congress.)

The longest remaining unbroken stretch of Route 66 begins at Exit 139 on Interstate 40 between Ashfork and Seligman and runs 162 miles to Topock. Seligman was originally known as Prescott Junction, founded in 1886 and later renamed for railroad financier Jesse Seligman. Interstate 40 opened on September 22, 1978, but the town refused to die.

The Bil-Mar-Den Motel had 44 units and was featured in a Ford commercial in the 1960s. Now the Stagecoach 66 Motel, the awesome sign is still in use. Seligman served as inspiration for the fictional town of Radiator Springs in the movie *Cars*. The community's preserved Route 66 heritage now makes it a popular tourist stop.

The Supai Motel at 134 East Chino Avenue opened in 1952 and takes its name from the nearby Havasupai Reservation. Advertised as "Seligman's newest and finest," it was owned and operated by Mr. and Mrs. H. Lanier and later by Mr. and Mrs. C. Van Ausdall. The renovated 15-room motel and its vintage sign still welcome travelers.

In 1953, Juan Delgadillo salvaged material from the railroad and built his drive-in with help from his brothers and father. Turned down by Dairy Queen, Juan signed with the Sno Cap chain. He delighted tourists with a menu offering "Dead Chicken," fake door handles, and a mustard bottle that squirted yellow string. Juan died on June 2, 2004. His family carries on the tradition. (Library of Congress.)

Angel Delgadillo opened a barbershop in his dad's old pool hall on May 22, 1950, and moved a few blocks to this location in 1972. Angel spearheaded the formation of the Historic Route 66 Association of Arizona in 1987, which started the Route 66 revival. Angel and his wife, Vilma, operate the Route 66 Gift Shop and Visitor's Center.

COURT DE LUXE

Seligman, Arizona

Steam Heat

The Court De Luxe was constructed in 1932 and is now the De Luxe Inn, the oldest motel still in operation in Seligman. Advertised as "new and fireproof," and "quiet, restful, attractively furnished," the Court De Luxe also offered closed garages and steam-heated rooms with or without tub or shower baths at "popular prices."

The Seligman Sundries building opened in 1904 and over the years has housed a theater, dance hall, and Ted's Trading Post and Soda Fountain. At one time, the building had the only telephone in Seligman. During the 1920s, cowboy actor Tom Mix stopped here. The building now houses Route 66 Historic Seligman Sundries.

The Havasu in Seligman was one of six Harvey Hotels in Arizona. It opened around 1905 and was named after the Havasupai tribe. It closed in 1954 and was used as offices by the Santa Fe before being abandoned and gutted. It was demolished in April 2008. The reading room now serves as a biology building at Seligman High School. (Mike Ward.)

Ethel Rutherford and her husband, who ran the Qumacho Café and Inn, opened the Copper Cart Restaurant in 1950. Louise Brown kept it going after Interstate 40 arrived. In February 1987, Angel Delgadillo called a meeting here that resulted in the organization of the Historic Route 66 Association of Arizona. The Copper Cart closed in 2008 but was remodeled and reopened a few months later.

Signs advertising the Hyde Park tourist camp west of Seligman invited travelers to "Park Your Hide at Hyde Park." For decades, Hyde Park offered the closest accommodations to Yampai/Coconino Caverns and was marked on road maps. Only the foundations of some buildings and a debris-filled swimming pool remain today. (Phillip Gordon.)

In 1927, Walter Peck was on his way to a poker game when he stumbled and nearly fell into a deep cave entrance. Peck used a winch to lower tourists into the cave, known as Yampai Caverns and then Coconino Caverns. A staircase was built in 1936. The name was changed to Dinosaur Caverns in 1957 and Grand Canyon Caverns in 1962.

The Peach Springs Trading Post predates Route 66. Note the swastikas. To the Navajos, the ancient "whirling log" was a sacred symbol. Imposed on an arrowhead, the swastika actually appeared on Arizona state highway markers until 1942. A new cobblestone trading post opened in 1929 and now houses the Hualapai Forestry Department.

HUALAPAI INDIAN COW BOYS   PEACH SPRINGS, ARIZONA

These Hualapai cowboys posed in front of the trading post building that was constructed in 1929. Peach Springs is the headquarters of the million-acre Hualapai Reservation. Hualapai means "People of the Tall Pine." Today the tribe operates a lodge in town, and Peach Springs is the gateway to the Hualapai Grand Canyon Skywalk.

Swedish immigrant John Osterman built his station after World War I. His brother Oscar bought it in 1925 and built the structure at right when Route 66 shifted a block away in 1931. Peach Springs was devastated when Interstate 40 opened 25 miles away in 1979. But this station, later owned by Robert Goldstein, was in business until 2007.

O! C. OSTERMAN AUTO COURT — PEACH SPRINGS, ARIZONA — U.S. ROUTE 66

Oscar Osterman constructed an auto court next to his station, charging $1 for a night in a wooden shack. He later built 16 attached units. Frank and Beatrice Boyd took over in 1938, and it became the Peach Springs Auto Court. After Frank died, Beatrice continued to operate the motel into the 1980s, but the buildings have since been demolished. (Mike Ward.)

Ethel Rutherford, who later became a state representative, operated the Qumacho Café with her husband. In 1949, the café was offering the Number Seven "Cattleman's Diet" breakfast for $2.78. It consisted of six eggs (any style), half a loaf of bread (toasted), a ham steak, potatoes, and "java till the pot runs dry." (Phillip Gordon.)

During his 1857 expedition, Lt. Edward Beale named a spring Truxton, which was his mother's maiden name. Truxton was little more than a railroad watering stop until Clyde McCune opened a service station and Donald Dilts opened a café in October 1951. But like these cars, many of the businesses were abandoned when Interstate 40 opened. (Library of Congress.)

Alice Wright opened the nine-room Frontier Motel at Truxton in 1952. Mildred Barker came to work in the Frontier's café in 1955 and took over the motel with her husband, Raymond, in 1970. The sign was recently restored with help from the Route 66 Association of Arizona and the Route 66 Corridor Management Program. (Library of Congress.)

The 7-V ranch and resort along Crozier Creek at Valentine was built by Ed Carrow and his six brothers beginning in 1924. The complex grew to include a restaurant, service station, garage, and eight cabins, as well as a large swimming pool. Route 66 was relocated after a flood in 1939, but the cabins still stand. (Steve Rider.)

The Hackberry General Store was originally the Northside Grocery and closed in 1978. Artist Bob Waldmire came to the abandoned store in 1992 and established his quirky International-Bioregional Old Route 66 Visitors Center. John and Kerry Pritchard took over in 1998. The store was featured in the films *Easy Rider* and *Roadhouse 66*. (Library of Congress.)

Eight

KINGMAN TO
COOL SPRINGS

In the days before auto air-conditioning, the giant flashing arrow sign blaring "Jugs Iced Free" was a welcome site for Route 66 travelers entering Kingman. The ice machine at Allen Bell's Flying A service station pumped out 450 pounds of ice cubes every day. The café was called the Tydway and was operated by Harry Tindel. (Bob Boze Bell.)

The Arizona Motel was located 3009–3023 East Andy Devine Avenue. The motel, with an attractive light turquoise brick exterior, advertised 14 modern units with tub and showers and the "Best for Less." It was owned and operated by Marjorie M. Ackerman when this view was made. The Rodeway Inn stands on this site today.

"The Very Finest Accomodations" were offered at the 25-room Pony Soldier Motel at 2939 Andy Devine Avenue. Mr. and Mrs. Tom White were the owners and operators at the time of this view. Advertised as the "Choicest Location in Kingman," it became the Route 66 Motel. The flashing arrow portion of the sign is still in use.

Bell's Motel, at 2030 East Andy Devine Avenue, was owned by Mr. and Mrs. Elza Bell. Other owners included Mr. and Mrs. Walter Beddow and Mr. and Mrs. James L. Richardson. Bell's Motel advertised "A fully modern, fire-proof, air-cooled motel." There were 13 units, and it still stands as the Desert Lodge Apartments.

The Hillcrest Motel, at 2018 Andy Devine Avenue, is still serving travelers today. AAA called it a "modest" court. It was advertised as "a new, fully modern, air-cooled motel with tile showers and electric heat" and consisted of 16 units. Owners included Earl and Ruth Chambers as well as Arlow and Gen Lamb.

City Cafe and Texaco Station, Kingman, Arizona

Roy Walker opened the City Café in 1943. William McCasland took over on March 5, 1945, and ran it for many years. The Texaco station was demolished when Andy Devine Avenue was widened. The City Café became the Hot Rod Café, but the building was torn down in 2009 to make room for a Walgreen's.

The Siesta Motel, at 1926 East Andy Devine Avenue, opened in 1929. Note the sign featuring a stereotypical image of a Mexican dozing beneath a cactus. The Siesta was operated by Mr. and Mrs. H. D. Wilbanks and was located across from the City Café. It is now the Siesta Apartments and Kitchenettes.

The Hilltop Motel at 1901 East Andy Devine Avenue advertised the "Best View in Kingman," overlooking the Hualapai Mountains. The 28-unit motel opened in 1954 and was operated by Jack and Erma Horner, later by Eleanor and George Allan, and by Louis and Charles Picard. The Hilltop Motel is still in business today.

John F. Miller knew a good deal when he saw one. In 1905, he bought a lot at First Street and Fremont Street in the dusty, isolated town of Las Vegas, Nevada. That site became Nevada Hotel, then the Hotel Sal Sagev (Las Vegas spelled backwards), and finally it grew into the Golden Gate Casino. When Hoover Dam was completed, Miller looked for Kingman to become an important crossroads, so he built the El Trovatore Motel in 1939.

After passing the Hilltop and El Trovatore Motels, Route 66/Andy Devine Avenue makes a steep descent through a rock cut into the Kingman business district. The TraveLodge chain operated a 32-unit motel at the bottom of the cut. It was later expanded to 38 rooms and is now operating as the Rambling Rose Motel.

The Brandin' Iron Motor Motel, later the Brandin' Iron Motel, was opened in 1953 by Mr. and Mrs. R. A. Bewley. Later owners included Mr. and Mrs. N. T. Gaylor and Hulan and Dixie Crawford. Advertised as "Kingman's Newest and Finest" when this view was made, the Branding Iron was demolished in 2001, and apartments were constructed on the site.

Charlie Lum came to Kingman from China in 1922 to work for his father at the White House Café. In 1951, he opened the Jade Restaurant and Cocktail Lounge, which he called the "Pride of Route 66." Charlie became a well-respected community leader, owning several other businesses. The vacant building still stands.

In 1938, the Arcadia Court opened at 909 Andy Devine Boulevard. Advertisements said it had the "finest appointments for the fastidious guest" and that Kingman has the "healthiest climate—no humidity and purest water." It grew to include 47 units. Frank and Susan Brace took over in 2001 and restored the property, now the Arcadia Lodge.

Opened in the early 1930s, the Gypsy Garden Auto Court was operated by Mr. and Mrs. Arthur Jones. Between 1949 and 1951, it was extensively modernized as shown here and became the Coronado Court. Stan Marbell operated the Coronado Court in the 1950s. The site in the 700 block of Andy Devine Avenue is now a vacant lot.

The Lockwood Café opened in 1937 and served "Chicken in the Rough," one of the first franchised foods. Beverly Osborne, a Route 66 restaurateur from Oklahoma City, came up with the idea of a chicken dinner eaten without silverware. The former cafe at 711 East Andy Devine Avenue is now St. Michael's Catholic Church.

Former Harvey Girl Clara Boyd opened her café in 1933. She and her husband, Jimmy, held a contest to rename the café, offering a coffee maker to the winner. Walter "Tuffy" Spaw came up with the name Casa Linda. The Casa Linda closed in 1964, and the building at 511 East Andy Devine Avenue now houses a surveying business. (Steve Rider.)

The Wal-A-Pai Motor Court, in the 600 block of Andy Devine Avenue, took its name from the phonetic pronunciation of Hualapai and used American Indian imagery to attract tourists. This card also added "Kingman is noted for its Mountain Spring Water, we have it iced." The court, with its 40 blue and white cottages, was demolished in 2007.

Constructed in 1935, Conrad Minka's White Rock Court was the cool place to stay. Minka drilled tunnels through solid rock into the mountain behind the motel, where he created an evaporative cooler with a water tank and burlap. Tunnels also connected the units with a central heater. Note the "Sleeping Dutchman" mountain.

Seen in this picture looking east on Front Street (now Andy Devine Avenue) at Fourth Street, the Keister's Kingman Drug Company Building was built in 1899. Lum Sing Yow's White House Café is to the right. The structures now house a restaurant. The banner promotes Kingman as educational and scenic, the "Gateway to Boulder Dam."

J. W. Thompson and John Mulligan built the Brunswick Hotel in 1909. They erected a wall creating two separate hotels after a dispute over a woman, whom Mulligan went on to marry. It is said to be haunted by the spirit of Mulligan's daughter, who fell down the stairs on her tricycle and died in 1920. Closed for two decades, the Brunswick was renovated in 1997, but it closed again in 2010.

The Old Trails Garage opened about 1914. Owners included Jasper Brewer, a county sheriff and state representative. During the 1920s, it advertised, "When we satisfy you we make a booster. Give us a try." A Packard repair facility was located here, and the towering sign from that era is being restored. (Jim Hinckley.)

Johanna and Harvey Hubbs ran a boardinghouse that was purchased by Thomas and Amy Devine in 1906. They renamed it the Hotel Beale in 1923, and then sold in 1926. Their son Andy Devine went on to fame as Guy Madison's sidekick in the *Wild Bill Hickok* television series. The Hotel Beale closed in 2000 and has fallen into disrepair. (Library of Congress.)

The Kimo Café and the adjoining Shell station at 105 East Andy Devine Avenue is now Mr. D'z Route 66 Diner, operated by Armando and Michelle Jimenez. Mr. D'z was in the spotlight in May 2006, when Oprah Winfrey visited and declared that the root beer was the world's best. The car is a 1940 Packard. (Jim Hinckley.)

The Desert Power and Water House, at far right, opened on July 31, 1907, and is the oldest reinforced concrete structure in Arizona. Electricity production ended in 1938. In 1997, the power house was converted into a visitor center housing an informative Route 66 museum and the Route 66 Association of Arizona's headquarters.

During World War II, over 20,000 bomber gunners trained at the Kingman Army Airfield. The airfield is shown here after the war, when it became a center for selling or scrapping thousands of military aircraft. One B-17 was sold to a Boy Scout troop for $350. The site became the Kingman Airport and Industrial Park.

Route 66 climbs into the Black Mountains west of Kingman, where N. R. Dunton ran a pipe to a spring 2 miles away and then established Cool Springs Camp in 1926. In 1936, James and Mary Walker took over and "rocked" the main building. Mary divorced James and married Floyd Slidell in 1939. The business thrived until the new highway opened in 1952.

Floyd and Mary would also be divorced, and Floyd was left to run the dying business with his niece and her husband. Cool Springs became a poultry operation called the Chicken Ranch. It was abandoned in 1964 and then burned down. Cool Springs was partly rebuilt in 1991 to be blown up for the film *Universal Soldier*. Ed Leuchtner bought it in 2002 and resurrected the landmark.

Nine

OATMAN TO TOPOCK

Prospector Lowell "Ed" Edgarton operated Ed's Camp. Tourists slept in their cars or pitched tents. One dollar rented a cot on a screened-in porch. That price also included free water, which otherwise was sold by the bucket. Ed became a well-known geologist and died in 1978. The camp and its lone saguaro cactus are still there.

Route 66 climbs 1,400 feet in 9 miles around hairpin curves with primitive stone and turnbuckle guardrails—that is if there are any guardrails at all. At 3,550 feet in elevation, the highway reaches Sitgreaves Pass, where the Summit Station and Ice Cream Parlor stood until 1967. Three states are visible from the summit.

The west side of the grade is not for the faint of heart, plunging 700 feet in 2 miles to Goldroad. The switchbacks can be seen in the 1959 movie *From Here to Eternity*. In the days of gravity-fed carburetors, locals would drive up the hill backwards. In the 1940s, service stations charged $3.50 to tow drivers too timid to tackle the grade.

Route 66 drops to the Gold Road Mine and the ruins of Goldroad. The boomtown sprouted when Jose Jerez discovered gold here in 1900. A government order closed the mines in 1942, and property owners leveled most of the town in 1949 to avoid paying taxes. The Goldroad Mine resumed operations in 1995 but closed in 1998.

Oatman is named for Olive Oatman, held captive for five years by American Indians after her family was massacred. The area population soared to 20,000 before the mines closed. New Route 66 bypassing Oatman opened on September 17, 1952. Within 24 hours, six of the seven gas stations in town had closed. The population fell to about 60.

Oatman now attracts 500,000 tourists annually. The old prospectors turned their burros loose when they were no longer needed. Their descendants now roam the streets freely, cadging carrots and leaving their calling cards on the wooden sidewalks. Colorful shops and cafés line the main street, and shots ring out from staged gunfights.

The Durlin Motel opened in 1902 and later became the Oatman Hotel. Clark Gable and Carol Lombard spent their honeymoon in room 15 on March 29, 1939. A ghost named Oatie, a miner who drank himself to death after his wife and children died, is said to haunt the hotel. Travelers can stay in Gable's or Oatie's rooms. (National Archives.)

In this view at Oatman, Elephant Tooth's Peak looms over the Tom Reed Gold Mine. In 1910, the Vivian Mine was about to close, and Oatman faced hard times. But Ely Hilty, Joe Anderson, and Daniel Tooker discovered this rich vein and launched a second boom. The government closed the mine in 1942, and only ruins remain.

The 1952 Route 66 alignment bypassing Oatman drops south from Kingman through the valley of the Sacramento Wash. At Yucca, establishments like the Joshua Motel and Café quickly sprang up to serve travelers on the new highway. The Joshua and nearly all of those businesses are now in ruins, killed off by Interstate 40.

A traveler's journey across Arizona on Route 66 comes to an end at Topock, Navajo for "many crossings." The community developed in 1883, as construction began on a wooden railroad bridge over the Colorado River. From 1890 until 1914, Joe and Nellie Bush operated the *Nellie T* ferry here. Today nothing remains of these structures.

The jagged peaks in the background gave the town of Needles, California, its name. The Needles were named by Lt. Amiel Weeks Whipple, who led the government railroad survey in 1854. In John Steinbeck's *The Grapes of Wrath*, Tom Joad said, "Never seen such tough mountains. This here's a murder country. This here's the bones of a country."

The steel Red Rock Railroad Bridge opened in 1890. Between 1914 and 1916, planks were laid over the rails and motorists paid a toll to cross between trains. A new railroad span opened in 1945, and the converted Red Rock Bridge began carrying Route 66 on May 21, 1947. Replaced by the Interstate 40 bridge in 1966, it was dismantled in 1976.

The graceful National Old Trails Arch Bridge opened on February 20, 1916. The bridge was featured in the motion picture *The Grapes of Wrath*. It was in danger of being demolished after traffic was shifted to the former railroad bridge but now carries a Pacific Gas and Electric natural gas pipeline across the Colorado River.

DISCOVER THOUSANDS OF LOCAL HISTORY BOOKS FEATURING MILLIONS OF VINTAGE IMAGES

Arcadia Publishing, the leading local history publisher in the United States, is committed to making history accessible and meaningful through publishing books that celebrate and preserve the heritage of America's people and places.

Find more books like this at
www.arcadiapublishing.com

Search for your hometown history, your old stomping grounds, and even your favorite sports team.